...Twelve Sopaipillas,
   Eleven Empanadas,
   Ten Biscochitos,
   Nine Flour Tortillas,
   Eight Bowls Posole,
   Seven Hunks O' Fudge,
   Six Bowls Natillas,
   Five Loaves O' Bread —
         Four Christmas Cakes,
         Three Chiles Rellenos,
         Two Chile Casseroles,
And an Applesauce Currant Cake.

miss you
Tom Teresa
Claire &
Nicole

For you
and your true love
Happy Holidays!

Printed in the United States of America
First Printing, 1991
ISBN 0-938513-10-9

AMADOR PUBLISHERS
P.O. Box 12335
Albuquerque, NM 87195 USA

RECIPES
FROM THE FAMILY OF
ADELA AMADOR

These recipes are simple, tasty, nutritious and easy to make.

What we have in New Mexico is a mixture of the Indian, Spanish/Mexican and Anglo, in the people and in the foods we prepare.

The traditional chile recipes of New Mexico have been enhanced by the addition from the Anglo culture of cheeses and sour cream.

Chile stew goes well with either sopaipillas or fresh bread. Either natillas, or Texas fudge, make an excellent dessert with any dinner. Both empanaditas and christmas cake are traditional, but not to be limited to the Holiday Season.

Enjoy, enjoy!

Adela Amador

SOPAIPILLAS

4 cups flour
3 teaspoons baking powder
3 tablespoons shortening
1 teaspoon salt
1¼ to 1½ cups water

Sift flour, baking powder and salt together. Cut in shortening; add water.

Roll out dough about ¼ inch thick and cut into 3-inch squares.

Deep fry until golden brown. Makes about 4 dozen.

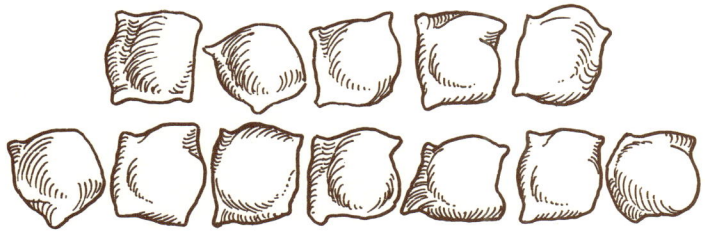

EMPANADITAS

Filling:
2 pounds cooked beef or 1 pound
each of beef and pork

2 cups prepared minced meat

½ cup piñon nuts (or chopped pecans)

½ teaspoon allspice

1 teaspoon nutmeg

¾ cup sugar

1 teaspoon salt

Boil meat until tender. Cool and grind fine.
Add minced meat, spices, nuts and sugar
until filling becomes thick and moist. If
filling is too dry add a little dark corn syrup.

Masa:
½ package yeast

3 cups lukewarm water

1½ tablespoons sugar

1½ teaspoons salt

1 egg

4 tablespoons pure lard

6 cups flour

Place yeast, sugar, salt in mixing bowl. Add water, and mix until dissolved.

Add beaten egg and melted lard, adding enough flour for a dry dough.

Roll out dough ⅛ inch thick, cut with round cookie cutter into discs about 4 inches in diameter.

Place 1 heaping teaspoon of filling in center of pattie. Fold over and pinch edges together so that dough will seal filling.

Deep fry until golden brown. Makes about 6 dozen.

BISCOCHITOS

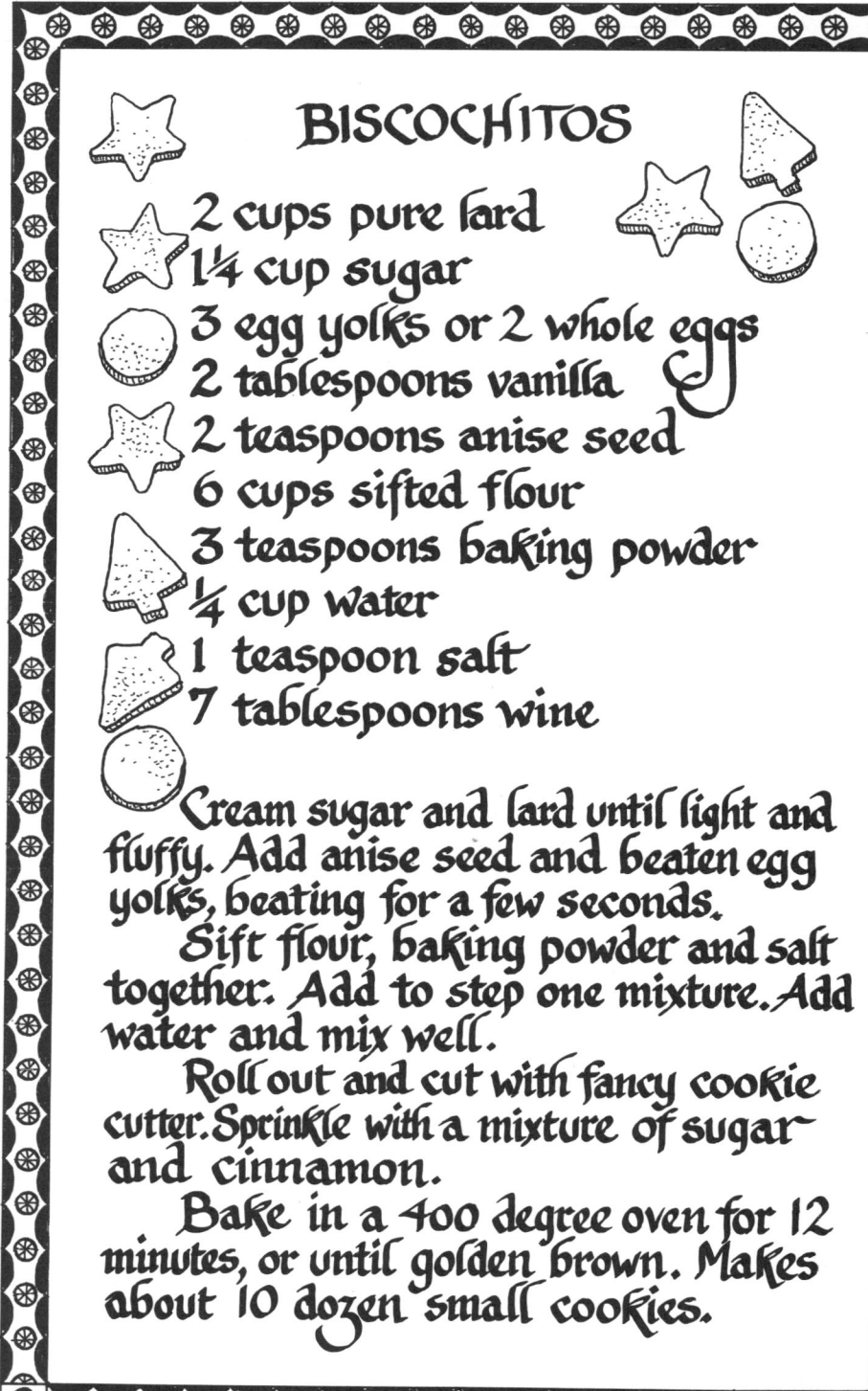

2 cups pure lard
1¼ cup sugar
3 egg yolks or 2 whole eggs
2 tablespoons vanilla
2 teaspoons anise seed
6 cups sifted flour
3 teaspoons baking powder
¼ cup water
1 teaspoon salt
7 tablespoons wine

Cream sugar and lard until light and fluffy. Add anise seed and beaten egg yolks, beating for a few seconds.

Sift flour, baking powder and salt together. Add to step one mixture. Add water and mix well.

Roll out and cut with fancy cookie cutter. Sprinkle with a mixture of sugar and cinnamon.

Bake in a 400 degree oven for 12 minutes, or until golden brown. Makes about 10 dozen small cookies.

FLOUR TORTILLAS

4 cups flour

2 teaspoons baking powder

4 tablespoons pure lard

1 ½ teaspoons salt

1 ½ cups warm water

Sift flour, baking powder and salt together. Add lard and water.

Knead dough until well mixed and form into balls about 3 inches in diameter.

Roll out into round flat shaped cakes about ⅛ inch thick and cook on griddle separately until both sides are spotted medium brown. Cook both sides. Makes about 1 dozen.

POSOLE

3 pounds pork cut in chunks

6 cups water

3 tablespoons red chile powder
or chile pods

½ teaspoon oregano

1 small onion

1 clove garlic, minced

6 cups prepared hominy

Boil meat 2½ hours until tender in the 6 cups water.

Add hominy and seasoning (oregano, onion, minced garlic and chile powder) to boiled meat and broth. Salt to taste. Simmer hominy and meat together for an additional ½ hour.

GREEN CHILE STEW

2 pounds pork cut in chunks

2 fresh tomatoes, or 1 pint of
               canned tomatoes

2 cups cubed potatoes

1 large chopped onion

2 cloves garlic, minced

2 cups chopped green chile

Boil meat until done, then add the remaining ingredients. Simmer for another ½ hour, or until potatoes are done.

TEXAS FUDGE

Bring to a boil:
- 2 cubes oleo
- 4 tablespoons cocoa
- 1 cup water

Mix:
- 2 cups sugar
- 2 cups flour
- 1 teaspoon vanilla
- ½ cup buttermilk
- 1 teaspoon soda

Bake in 9x12 pan at 375 degrees for 35 minutes.

Ten minutes before cake is done, make frosting

Boil:
- ¼ pound oleo
- 4 tablespoons cocoa
- ¼ cup water
- 2 teaspoons milk

Add:
  1 pound powdered sugar
  1 teaspoon vanilla

Add:
  1 cup coconut, or 1 cup chopped
                    nuts, or both

Spread on top of cake after baking.

NATILLAS
(MILK CUSTARD)

1 pint milk

¼ teaspoon salt

2 tablespoons flour

1 teaspoon vanilla

2 eggs

½ cup sugar

Beat yolks and add to sugar, flour and salt. Add to hot milk and boil until it thickens. Add vanilla. Beat egg whites until stiff and fold into the natillas. This serves 4. Sprinkle with cinnamon.

FRESH BREAD (REAL BREAD)

Use any kind of flour or mixture of dark and white flour. We add 2 cups of wheat germ to white flour.

3 pints warm water

4 packages yeast

6 tablespoons oil

9 tablespoons sugar

3 tablespoons salt

2 eggs

Add about 12 cups flour, or enough to make a soft (not sticky) dough. Let rise in warm place until volume doubles. Knead and let rise again. Make into loaves or rolls and place in well-greased pans. Let rise again. Bake at 400 degrees for 20 to 25 minutes.

CHRISTMAS CAKE

1 cup butter
2 cups sugar
4 eggs
4 cups sifted flour
1 teaspoon soda
½ teaspoon salt
1½ cups buttermilk
1 tablespoon grated orange rind
1 cup chopped pecans
1 8oz. package dates, chopped

Cream together sugar and butter. Beat eggs and add to butter and sugar. Beat together. Sift together flour, soda and salt. Add to creamed mixture, alternating with buttermilk. Add orange rind, dates and pecans. Pour into greased and floured tube pan. Bake at 325° for 1½ hours. While still hot, before removing from pan, punch many holes in cake all the way to the bottom with ice pick.

Glaze:

- 1 cup orange juice
- 2 cups sugar
- 2 tablespoons grated orange rind

Dissolve sugar and orange juice in small saucepan over heat. Do not boil. Add orange rind.

Pour hot glaze over cake. Let the glaze drip into holes in cake. If cake has not pulled away from sides and tube, loosen with a knife, so that some of the glaze runs down sides and center of cake. Let cake stand in pan for several hours. Cake must be entirely cool before removing from pan. Decorate top of cake with pecans as desired.

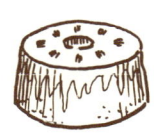

CHILES RELLENOS

8 to 12 roasted and peeled green chiles

½ pound longhorn cheese

½ cup flour

½ teaspoon garlic salt

2 eggs

De-seed chile and fill with either grated or sliced cheese. Mix together flour and salt and roll each chile in mixture. Beat eggs well. Dip chile in egg and fry in hot oil until golden brown.

GREEN CHILE CASSEROLE

4 cups boiled chicken, cut up

2 cans green chile, chopped

1 chopped onion

2 cans cream of chicken soup

1 can milk, or water

1 dozen corn tortillas

2 cups grated cheese (cheddar is best)

Saute chopped onions and add chicken, chile, soup and milk. Fry tortillas in oil until soft (a very short time!). Place chicken mixture in bottom of 9 x 12 pan. Cover with three or four tortillas. Cover with cheese and cover with chicken mixture. Repeat layers until mixture is used up. Last layer should be cheese. Bake at 350 degrees for 30 minutes.

APPLESAUCE CURRANT CAKE

3 cups sugar (1½ cup brown, 1½ cup white)
½ cup oleo
2 eggs
½ teaspoon salt
2 cups flour
2 teaspoons soda
1 teaspoon vanilla
2 cups unsweetened applesauce
1½ cups currants
1 teaspoon cinnamon
1 teaspoon allspice

Mix first four ingredients together. Add flour. Mix applesauce and soda together, add to previous mixture. Add remaining ingredients and mix. Bake in a 9 x 12 pan for 35 minutes at 350 degrees.

Melt ½ stick oleo. Add:
- 1 cup brown sugar
- 4 tablespoons milk
- dash of salt

Bring to a boil. Remove from heat and add:
- 1 teaspoon vanilla
- ½ cup chopped nuts

Pour over cake and place under broiler for one minute.

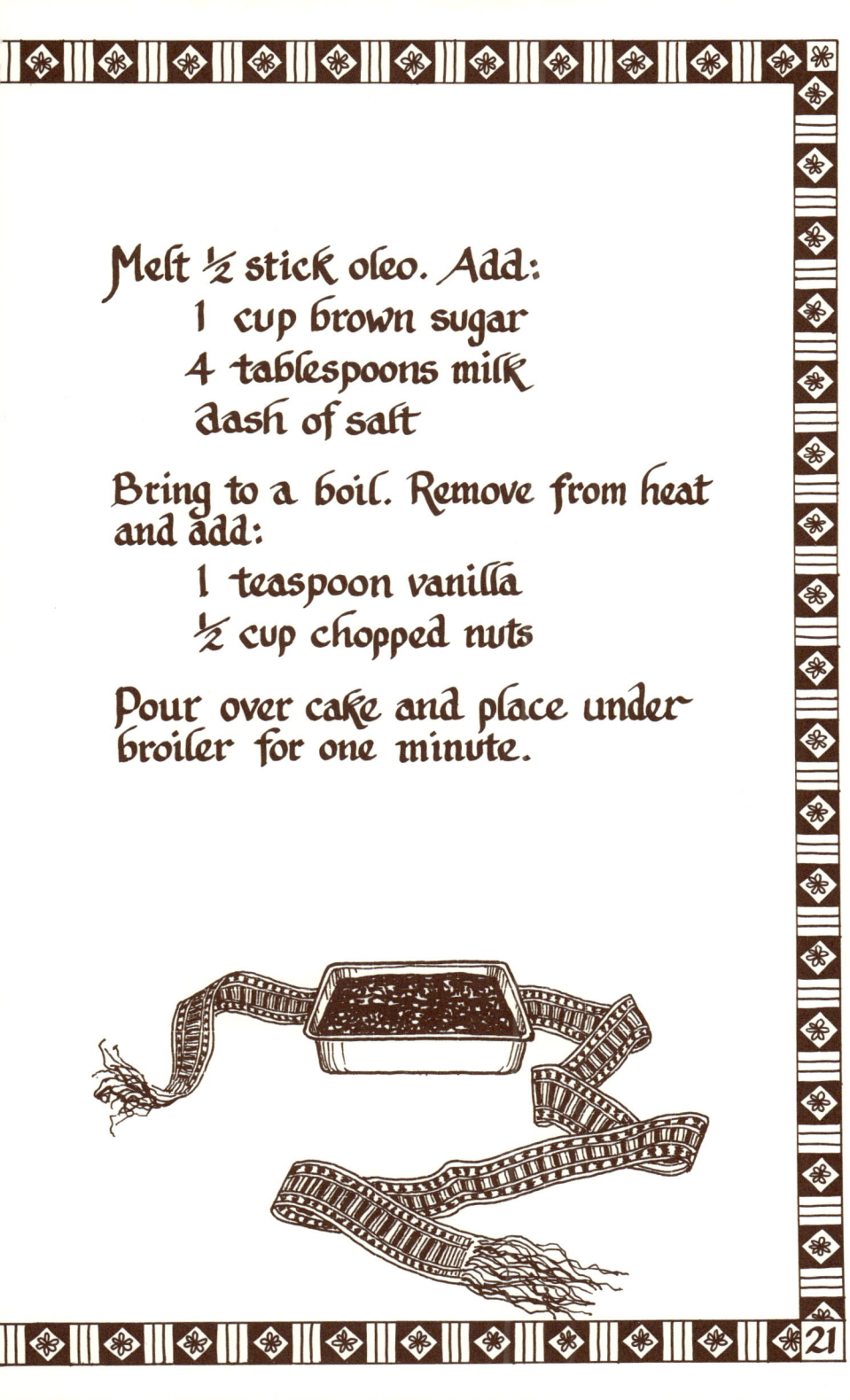

NO-SALT
TRUTH-SERUM
MARGARITA

2 6 oz. cans frozen limeade

Use same limeade can to measure the following:

2 cans water

1 can triple sec

2 cans Gold tequila

Mix and serve over ice cubes. Makes 10 4 oz. drinks.
Be careful how you use it.

More Fine Southwestern Fare from Amador Publishers:

CAESAR OF SANTA FE: A NOVEL FROM HISTORY, by Tim MacCurdy

Colonial New Mexico around 1640 . . . The exploits of Governor Luis de Rosas . . . Intrigue, treachery, a tempestuous love affair . . . A rousing adventure discovered by a historian, and retold by the same master story teller. (240 pp.)

"It should become one of our classics."
—Tony Hillerman

SOULS AND CELLS REMEMBER: A LOVE STORY, by Harry Willson

A journey "back East" and back in time . . . Intercultural conflict, anger and ancient longings, sexual understanding, love and reincarnation—a Pueblo Indian "time/travel romance." (188 pp.)

"A dream you would like to have come true for yourself."
—Silver Ravenwolf

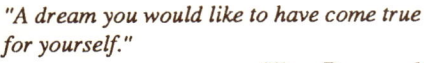

CROSSWINDS: A SOUTHWEST NOVEL, by Michael A. Thomas

A darkly comic modern western, celebrating the land, the people and the language . . . Strong women, red-necks, ex-hippies, wetbacks and fundamentalists, and our hero who develops from a foul-mouthed impulsive loser into a sane hard-working citizen. (169 pp.)

"Very funny, very convincing novel of the Great Southwest."
—THE ALBUQUERQUE JOURNAL

HUMMINGBIRD BRIGADE:
A NOVEL OF HEALING
by David L. Condit

Each member of a tragi-comic quartet rebounds from personal loss and pain into a shared resolve to break the chain of abuse . . . Celebrates the healing power of the Land of Enchantment. (165 pp.)

"Brings to life the motivations that begat a spontaneous social and spiritual movement, that much-abused exquisitely painful era, the premytholgical Sixities."
—WILDERNESS OUTLOOK

DUKE CITY TALES:
ALBUQUERQUE SHORT STORIES
by Harry Willson

Luminarias, balloons, peace protests, cops, reporters, litter, DWI, stray dogs and a fumbling old alchemist whose attempts to bring about his goal of "peace and quiet" are comical and less than satisfactory, giving pause to those of us who feel called upon to change the world . . . (169 pp.)
"A light touch of humor . . . creative tales and endearing characters."
—NEW MEXICO ENGLISH JOURNAL

# OF COPIES	ORDER BLANK		COST
———— THE HUMMINGBIRD BRIGADE	@	8.00	————
———— CROSSWINDS	@	8.00	————
———— CAESAR OF SANTA FE	@	9.00	————
———— A WORLD FOR THE MEEK	@	9.00	————
———— TAIL TIGERSWALLOW . . .	@	8.00	————
———— SOULS AND CELLS REMEMBER	@	8.00	————
———— THE CARLOS CHADWICK MYSTERY	@	9.00	————
———— DUKE CITY TALES	@	8.00	————
———— EVA'S WAR Paperback	@	9.00	————
———— EVA'S WAR Hardcover	@	17.00	————
———— TWELVE GIFTS	@	3.00	————

NM Residents add 5.75% sales tax: ════════

Total ————————

Send to: Name ————————————————————

Address ————————————————————

City, State, Zip ————————————————